Anonymous

The Bold Soldier Boy's Song Book

Vol. 1

Anonymous

The Bold Soldier Boy's Song Book
Vol. 1

ISBN/EAN: 9783337309220

Printed in Europe, USA, Canada, Australia, Japan

Cover: Foto ©Thomas Meinert / pixelio.de

More available books at **www.hansebooks.com**

THE VIRGINIAN'S SONG OF HOME.

Virginia! Virginia! my home far away,
Dear land of my birth, how I long for the day,
When my wand'rings shall cease and my footsteps once more
Shall turn to the scenes that I love and adore;
Virginia! Virginia! my dear native home!
I ne'er will forget thee wherever I roam!
Virginia! Virginia! my dear native home!
I ne'er will forget thee wherever I roam!

Virginia! Virginia! thou glorious old State,
The home of the valiant, the good and the great;
Whose sons in the front of the battle have stood,
And in Liberty's cause poured out their life's blood,
The annals are filled with their deeds of renown!
Their names are the jewels that shine in thy crown!

Virginia! oh! ne'er may thy sons see the day
When thy glory shall wane or thy ____ all decay;
But long may thy banner wave proudly on high,
And "SIC SEMPER TYRANNIS" be ever their cry;
May thy patriot sons bid the nations afar
Render homage and praise to Virginia's Star!

SWEET SIXTEEN.

DAUGHTER.

"To-morrow, Ma, I'm sweet sixteen,
  And Billy Grimes, the drover,
Has popped the question to me, Ma,
  And wants to be my lover
To-morrow morn, he says, Mamma,
  He's coming here quite early,
To take a pleasant walk with me
  Across the field of barley."

MOTHER.

" Tou must not go, my daughter dear,
    There's no use now a talking,
You shall not go across the field
    With Billy Grimes a walking;
To think of his presumption, too,
    The dirty, ugly drover!
I wonder where your pride has gone,
    To think of such a rover."

DAUGHTER.

"Old Grimes is dead, you know, Mamma,
    And Billy is so lonely!
Besides, they say of Grimes' estate,
    That Billy is the only
Surviving heir to all that's left,
    And that they say is nearly
A good ten thousand dollars, Ma,
    About six hundred yearly!"

MOTHER.

"I did not hear, my daughter dear,
    Your last remark quite clearly;
But Billy is a clever lad,
    And no doubt loves you dearly;
Remember, then, to-morrow morn,
    To be up bright and early,
To take a pleasant walk with him
    Across the field of barley."

BOWLD SOGER BOY.

Oh there's not a trade that's going,
Worth showing, or knowing,
Like that from glory growing,
    For a bowld soger boy!
Where right or left we go.
Sure you know, friend or foe,
Will have the hand or toe
    From the bowld soger boy!
There's not a town we marched thro
But ladies looking arch thro'
The window pan s wil sa ch thro'

The ranks to find their joy,
While up the street, each girl you meet,
With look so sly, will cry "My eye!
Oh isn't he a darling, -
    The bowld soger boy."

But when we get the rout,
How they pout and they shout,
While to the right about
    Goes the bowld soger boy.
'Tis then the ladies fair,
In despair, tear their hair,
But the divil a one I care,
    Says the bowld soger boy!
For the world is all before us,
Where the landladies adore us,
And ne'er refuse to score us,
    But chalk us up with joy.
We taste her tap, we tear her cap,
" Oh that's the chap for me," says she.
" Oh isn't he a darling,
    The bowld soger boy."

Then come along with me,
Gramachree, and you'll see
How happy you will be
    With your bowld soger boy.
Faith if you are up to fun,
With a run, 'twill be done,
In the snapping of a gun,
    Says the bowld soger boy.
And 'tis then that without scandal,
Myself will proudly dandle
The little farthing candle
    Of our mutual flame, my joy!
May his light shine as bright as mine
'Til in the line he'll blaze, and raise
The glory of his corps,
    Like a bowld soger boy!

SOLDIER'S RETURN.

When wild war's deadly blast was blown,
    And gentle peace returning,
Wi' mony a sweet babe fatherless,

And mony a widow mourning,
I left the lines and tented field,
Where lang I'd been a lodger,
My humble knapsack all my wealth,
A poor but honest sodger.

A leal, light heart was in my breast,
My hand unstained wi' plunder,
And for fair Scotia hame again,
I cheery on did wander.
I thought upon the banks o' Coil,
I thought upon my Nancy,
I thought upon the witching smile
That caught my youthful fancy.

At length I reached the bonnie Glen,
Where early life I sported,
I passed the mill and twisting thorn,
Where Nancy aft I courted ;
Who spied I but my ain dear maid,
Down by her mother's dwelling ?
And turned me round to hide the flood
That in my e'e was swelling.

Wi' altered voice, quoth I, "Sweet lass,
Sweet as yon hawthorn's blossom,
Oh happy, happy may he be
That's dearest to thy bosom !
My purse is light, I've far to gang,
And fain would be thy lodger ;
I've served my king and country long,
Take pity on a sodger.'

Sae wistfully she gazed on me,
And lovelier was than ever,
Quoth she, "A sodger once I loved ;
Forget him shall I never :
Our humble cot and hamely fair,
Ye freely shall partake it ;
That gallant badge, the dear cockade,
Ye're welcome for the sake o't."

She gazed,—she reddened like a rose—
Syne pale as ony lily,
She sank within my arms and cried
"Art thou my ain dear Willie ?"

By Him who made yon sun and sky,
  By whom true love's regarded,
I am the man; and thus may still
  Tr ue lovers be rewarded.

"The wars are o'er, and I'm come hame,
  And find thee still true hearted;
'Tho poor in gear, we're rich in love,
  And mair we'se ne'er be parted."
Quoth she, "My grand-ire left me gold,
  A mailen* plenished fairly:
And come my faithful sodger lad,
  Thou'rt welcome to it dearly."

For gold the merchant ploughs the main,
  The farmer ploughs the manor;
But glory is the sodger's prize,
  The sodger's wealth is honor:
The brave poor sodger ne'er despise,
  Nor count him a- a stranger;
Remember he's our country's stay,
  In day and hour of danger.

BRIGHTEST EYES.

Thou'st pearls and diamonds fair one,
Hast all that men adore,
And hast the brightest eyes, love,
My dearest, what would thou have more?
Thou hast the brightest eyes love,
My dearest, what would'st thou have more?

With thy bright eyes thou'st pain'd me,
Man ne er was so tortured before,
Down down to despair thou hast brought me,
My dearest, what would'st thou have more?
With thy brightest eyes thou'st pain'd me,
My dearest, what would'st thou have more?

These beauteous eyes of thine, love,
I've sung them o'er and o'er,
In countless songs immortal.
My dearest what would'st thou have more?
In countless songs immortal.
My dearest what would'st thou have more?

*Farm.

KATY DARLING.

Oh, they tell me thou art dead, Katy Darling,
  That thy smile I may never more behold!
Did they tell thee I was false, Katy Darling,
  Or my love for thee had e'er grown cold?
Oh, they knew not the loving
  Of the hearts of Erin's sons,
When a love like to thine, Katy Darling,
  Is the goal to the race he runs.
    Oh hear me, sweet Katy,
For the wild flowers greet me, Katy Darling,
  And the love-birds are singing on each tree;
Wilt thou never more hear me, Katy Darling?
  Behold, love, I'm waiting for thee.

I'm kneeling by thy grave, Katy Darling,
  This world is all a blank world to me;
Oh could'st thou hear my wailings, Katy Darling,
  Or, think, love, I am sighing for thee!
Oh, methinks the stars are weeping,
  By their soft and lambent light,
And thy heart would be melting, Katy Darling,
  Could'st thou see thy lone Dermot this night.
    Oh, listen, sweet Katy,
For the wild flowers are sleeping, Katy Darling,
  And the love-birds are nestling in each tree;
Wilt thou never more hear me, Katy Darling,
  Or know, love, I'm kneeling by thee?

'Tis useless all my weeping, Katy Darling,
  But I'll pray that thy spirit be my guide,
And that when my life is spent, Katy Darling,
  They will lay me down to rest by thy side.
Oh a huge great grief I'm bearing,
  Though I scarce can heave a sigh;
And I'll ever be dreaming, Katy Darling,
  Of thy love every day 'till I die.
For the wild flowers are sleeping, Katy Darling,
  And the love-birds are nestling in each tree;
Wil't thou never more hear me, Katy Darling,
  Or know, love, I'm kneeling by thee?

BRUCE'S ADDRESS.

Scots, wha hae wi' Wallace bled,
Scots, wham Bruce has often led;
  Welcome to your gory bed,
    Or to victory.

Now's the day, and now's the hour;
See the front of battle lower;
See approach proud Edward's power—
   Chains and slavery!

Wha will be a traitor knave?
Wha can fill a coward's grave?
Wha sae base as be a slave?
   Let him turn and flee!

Wha for Scotland's King and law
Freedom's sword will strongly draw,
Freeman stand, or freeman fa'?
   Let him follow me!

By oppression's woes and pains!
By your sons in servile chains!
We will drain our dearest veins
   But they shall be free!

Lay the proud usurper low!
Tyrants fall in every foe!
Liberty's in every blow!
   Let us do or die!

WE MET!

We met, 'twas in a crowd—
  And I thought he would shun me;
He came—I could not breathe,
  For his eye was on me;
  —his words were cold,
  his smile was unaltered;
I knew how much he felt, for his deep-toned voice falter'd!
  I wore my ████ robe ████ I rival'd its whit████
Bright gems ████████ in my ████;
  How I hate ████████ ████
He called ██████ ████ ████—
  As ████████████ another;
Oh! ████████ ██ the ████ of this ████████ ██████

████████ we met, and a fair girl ████
████ ████ whispered her, as I once ████ ████ ██
████ upon his arm—once twice more ████ e only—
████ for I deserved to feel ████—I ████ ██——
████ knew ██ be his bride! at the ████ h ██ give her
████ 'that ████████ pure for a ████thless ████iver;
  The world may think me gay, for my feelings I smother;
Oh! thou hast been the cause of this anguish, my Mother!

ALL HAIL TO THE BRAVE AND FREE!

All hail! to the brave and free,
On land or on rolling sea,
Whose hosts advance, with sword and lance,
In the cause of liberty;
And whether in triumph's car,
They follow vict'ry's star,
Or patriots fall 'neath glory's pall,
They still are the pri e of war.
Then hail! to the brave and free,
On land and rolling sea,
With hosts advance, with sword and lance,
In the cause of liberty.

Oh! who on the rolls of fame
Shall boast of the brightest name?
Or who shall bear, from woman fair,
Those smiles which the world claim?
For whom shall the song arise
Which the people send the skies?
For whom shall bloom, on battle tomb,
The laurel whic . never dies?
Oh! none but the brave and free,
On land or on rolling sea,
Whose hosts advance, with sword and lance,
In the cause of liberty.

Then raise our flag on high!
A meteor gainst the sky!
With rolling drum, we'll proudly come,
To guard it or to die.
Firm place the lance in rest,
Against a faithful breast,
The trumpets call, obey we all,
And valor shall do the best.
And then with the brave and free,
On land r on rolling sea,
Whose hosts advance, with sword and lance,
We'll sing of the victory.

NO, NE'R CAN THY HOME BE MINE.

I have told thee how sweet the roses are
In my home beyond the sea.
Where the dark eyed maid, with sweet guitar,
Sits under the orange tree;

Then fly, oh fly from this isle of storm,
  Where all that is fair must pine,
To a sky more blue and a sun more warm—
  Henceforth let my home be thine.

I have heard thee tell of a sky more blue
  And a sun more warm than this;
And I sometimes thought, if thy tale be true,
  To dwell in that clime of bliss;
But oh! when I gaze on my tranquil cot,
  Where clematis boughs entwine,
The land of the stranger tempts me not;
  No, ne'er can thy home be mine.

I will sing to thee, if thou wilt rove,
  The songs of the olden time;
Thou wilt never compare with my ardent love,
  The love of a colder clime;
Thou wilt scorn the fruits of thy mountain home,
  Beholding the purple vine;
Then come to the land of my birth, oh! come—
  Henceforth let my home be thine.

Alas! 'tis plain that my mountain home
  Must ever be scorned by thee;
And may I not fear that a time will come
  When thou wilt have scorn for me?
And oh! there is one who loves me here,
  Whose voice, if less sweet than thine,
To my simple taste is far more dear—
  No, ne'er can thy home be mine.

Take me home to the place where I loved first
  The sunny south side the home,
Wh   ng bird   to rest
         I tempted to
         et of the dear home I left—
         hearts that sheltered me then—
         d dear ones of whom I'm bereft,
      r the old place again.
         me to the place where my little ones sleep,
         lies buried close by,
      e graves of the loved ones I long to weep,
  And among them to rest when I die.

Take me home to the place where the orange trees grow,
  To my cot in the ever-green shade,
Where the flowers on the river's green margin may blow
  Their sweets on the bank where we played.
The path to our cottage they say has grown green,
  And the place is quite lonely around.
And I know that the smiles and the forms I have seen
  Now lie deep in the dark mossy ground.
    Take me home to the place where the little ones sleep,
      Poor massa lies buried close by,
    O'er the graves of the loved ones I long to weep,
      And among them to rest when I die.

Take me home, let me see what is left that I knew:
  Can it be that the old house is gone?
The dear friends of my childhood indeed must be few,
  And I must lament all alone.
But yet I'll return to the place of my birth,
  Where my children have played at the door,
Where they pulled the white blossoms that garnished the earth
  Which will echo their footsteps no more.
    Take me home to the place where my little ones sleep,
      Poor massa lies buried close by,
    O'er the graves of the loved ones I long to weep,
      And I sigh for the old place again.

ERIN IS MY HOME.

O, I have _____ in many lands,
  And many fr____ I've met;
Not one ____ sce__ ___ kindly smile
  Can th__ fond h___ fo____;
____ c____ th__ in content;
____ re I wish to roam;
____ my back to Erin's isle,
____ is my home.

____ were my place of b__th,
____ her tranquil shore;
____ Columbia were my home,
____ ____ I'd adore;
____ pleasant dare in both I p____
____ of days to come;
O____ my back to Erin's isle,
For ____ is my home.

SHELLS OF OCEAN.

One summer eve, with pensive though*,
  I wandered on the sea-beat shore,
Where oft i heedless infant sport,
  I gather'd shells in days before,
  I gather'd shells in days before.
The plashing waves like music fell,
  Responsive to my fancy wild,
A dream came o'er me like a spell,
  I thought I was again a child,
A dream came o'er me like a spell,
  I thought I was again, again a child.

I stooped upon the pebbly strand
  To cull the toys that round me lay;
But as I took them in my hand,
  I threw them one by one away.
Oh! thus, I said, in ev'ry stage
  By toys our fancy is beguiled,
We gather shells from youth to age,
  And then we leave them like a child.

———

BONNY JEAN.

O! the summer morn is brightly glowing,
  The wild birds ...... their song;
And the st.......... ly murmurs,
  So gentl............
Where th.................... ing;
  In th.....
Ther.....
.... the r... ti...
.... bird's jo...
.... soft an.............sic
.... my heart t...
'Th............ that beams...
'M............ 'ry scenes...
While I ...... ly wander
  With ... heart's true ...
My bonny, bonny Jean.

THE OLD CANOE.

Where the rocks are gray and the shore is steep,
And the waters below look dark and deep,
Where the rugged pine in its lonely pride,
Leans gloomily over the murky tide;
Where the reeds and rushes are tall and rank,
Where the weeds grow thick on the winding bank;
Where the shadow is heavy the whole day through,
Lies at its mooring the old canoe.

The useless paddles are idly dropped,
Like a sea-bird's wings that the storm hath lopped,
And crossed on the railing, one o'er one,
Like folded hands when the work is done;
While busily back and forth between,
The spider stretches his silvery screen,
And the solemn owl with his dull "too-hoo,"
Nestles down on the side of the old canoe.

The stern, half sunk in the slimy wave,
Rots slowly away in its living grave,
And the green moss creeps o'er its dull decay,
Hiding the mouldering dust away,
Like the hand that plants o'er the tomb a flower,
Or the ivy that mantles a fallen tower;
While many a blossom of liveliest hue,
Springs up o'er the stern of the old canoe.

The currentless waters are dead and still—
But the light winds play with the boat at will,
And lazily in and out again
It floats the length of its rusty chain,
Like the weary thoughts of time,
That meet and mingle in rude chime,
And the shallow turn anew,
By the drifting the old canoe.

O, many a careless hand,
I have pushed from the pebbly strand,
And paddled where the stream ran quick;
When the waters wild and the storm was thick;
And laughed o'er the rocking side,
And looked below in the broken tide,
To see that the faces and boats were two,
That were mirrored back from the old canoe.

But now as I lean o'er the crumbling side,
And look below in the sluggish tide,
The face that I see is graver grown,
And the laugh that I hear has a sober tone,
And the hands that lent to the light skiff wings,
Have grown familiar with sterner things;
But I love to think of the hours that flew,
As I rocked where the whirl's their wild spray threw;
Ere the blossoms moved or the green grass grew,
O'er the mouldering stern of the old canoe.

THE SOUTHERN GIRL'S SONG.

AIR—"*Bonnie Blue Flag.*"

Oh, yes, I am a Southern girl,
    I glory in the name,
And boast it with far greater pride,
    Than glittering wealth or fame.
I envy not the Northern girl,
    Her robe of beauty rare,
Though diamonds grace her snowy neck.
    And pearls bedeck her hair.
Hurrah, hurrah, for the Sunny South, so dear,
Three cheers for the homespun dress that Southern ladies wear.

This homespun dress is plain, I know,
    My hat's palmetto, too;
But then it shows what Southern girls
    For Southern rights will do.
We've sent the bravest of our land
    To battle with the foe,
And we would give a helping hand,
    We love them so, you know.
Hurrah, hurrah, for the Sunny South, so dear,
Three cheers for the homespun dress that Southern ladies wear.

Now Northern goods are out of date,
    And since old Abe's blockade,
We Southern girls will be content
    With goods that's Southern made.
We scorn to wear a bit of lace,
    A bit of Northern silk;
But make our homespun dresses up,
    And wear them with much grace.
Hurrah, hurrah, for the Sunny South, so dear,
Three cheers for the homespun dress that Southern ladies wear.

The Southern land's a glorious land,
　And her's a glorious cause,
Then here's three cheers for Southern rights
　And for the Southern boys.
We have sent our sweethearts to the war,
　But, dear girls, never mind,
Your soldier love will not forget
　The girls he left behind.
Hurrah, hurrah, for the Sunny South, so dear,
Three cheers for the sword and plume that Southern soldiers wear.

　A soldier lad is the lad for me,
　　A brave heart I adore.
　And when the Sunny South is free,
　　And fighting is no more,
　I will choose me then a lover brave
　　From out that gallant band,
　The soldier lad I love the best
　　Shall have my heart and hand.
Hurrah, hurrah, for the Sunny South, so dear,
Three cheers for the sword and plume that Southern soldiers wear.

　And now, young man, a word to you,
　　If you would win the fair,
　Go to the field where honor calls
　　And win your lady there.
　Remember that our brightest smiles
　　Are for the true and brave,
　And that our tears fall for the one
　　Who fills a soldier's grave.
Hurrah, hurrah, for the Sunny South, so dear,
Three cheers for the sword and plume that Southern soldiers wear.

BANKS OF ALLAN WATER.

On the banks of Allan Water,
　When the sweet spring time did fall,
Was the miller's lovely daughter,
　The fairest of them all.
For his bride a soldier sought her,
　And a winning tongue had he,
On the banks of Allan Water,
　None was so gay as she.

On the banks of Allan Water,
  When brown autumn spreads its stors,
Then I saw the miller's daughter,
  But she smiled no more;
For the summer grief had brought her,
  And the soldier false was he,
On the banks of Allan Water,
  None was so sad as she.

On the banks of Allan Water,
  When the winter snow fell fast,
Still was seen the miller's daughter,
  Chilling blew the blast.
But the miller's lovely daughter.
  Both from cold and care was free,
On the bank of Allan Water,
  There a corpse lay she.

AH! I HAVE SIGHED TO REST ME.

Ah! I have sighed to rest me
  Deep in the quiet grave—
    Sighed to rest me,
  But all in vain I crave;
Oh! fare thee well, my Leonora, fare thee well!
  Ah! I have sighed for rest!
    Yet all in vain do I crave—
Oh! fare thee well, my Leonora, fare thee well!

Out of the love I bear thee,
  Yield I my life for thee;
    Wilt thou think—
  Wilt thou me.....ne?
Oh think of me.....nora, fare thee well!
  Out of the love I bear thee,
    Yield I my life for thee;
      Ah! think of me!
  Ah! think of me, my Leonora, fare thee well!

  Though I no more behold thee,
    Yet is thy name a spell,
  Yet is thy name, yet is thy name a spell,
Cheering my last lone hour, Leonora, farewell!

COMIN' THRO' THE RYE.

Gin a body m et a body
　Comin' thro' the.rye,
Gin a body kiss a body,
　Need a body cry ?
Ilka lassie has a laddie,
　Ne'er a 'ane hae I ;
But all the lads they love me well,
　And what the waur am I.

Gin a body meet a body
　Comin' frae the well,
Gin a body kiss a body,
　Need a body tell ?
Ilka lassie has a laddie,
　Ne'er a 'ane hae I ;
But all the lads they love me well,
　And what the waur am I.

Gin a body meet a body
　Comin' fra the town,
Gin a body kiss a body,
　Need a body frown ?
Ilka Jennie has her Jockey,
　Ne'er a 'ane hae I ;
But all the lads they smile on me
　Comin' thro' the rye.

COME, SOLDIERS, COME—'TIS THE ROLLING DRUM.

Come, soldiers, come—'tis the rolling drum—
　And is heard the ；
Mount while you ma th speed away
　Where the battle r .
　　Draw each trusty blade
　　From its scabbard shade ;
With vengeance charge the blow,
　　Till from hill and glen,
　　Mossy brake and fen,
Is banished the craven foe.

The rosy dawn o'er the verdant lawn
　Now pours out her radiant flood ;
Yet the setting sun, ere the fight be done,

Shall shine on our 'oeman's blood,
　Then poise the lance,
　To the charge advance,
Let the purple torrent flow,
　Till from hill and glen,
　Mossy brake and fen,
Is banished the craven foe.

WIDOW MACHREE.

Widow Machree, it's no wonder you frown,
　Och, hone! widow Machree—
Faith, it ruins your looks, that same dirty black gown,
　Och, hone! widow Machree.
　　How altered you are
　　With that close cap you wear,
　　'Tis destroying your hair,
　Which should be flowing free;
　　Be no longer a churl,
　　Of its black silken curl,
　Och, hone! widow Machree.

Widow Machree, now the summer is come,
　Och, hone! widow Machree.
When everything smiles should a beauty look glum?
　Och, hone! widow Machree;
　　See, the birds go in pairs,
　　And the rabbits and hares,
　　Why, even the bears
　Now in couples agree;
　　And the mute little fish,
　　Tho' they can't spake their wish—
　Och, hone! widow Machree.

Widow Machree, and when winter comes in,
　Och, hone! widow Machree,
To be poking the fire all alone is a sin,
　Och, hone! widow Machree.
　　Why, the shovel and tongs
　　To each other belongs,
　　And the kettle sings songs
　Full of family glee;
　　While alone with your cup
　　Like a hermit you sup,
　Och, hone! widow Machree.

2

And how do you know with the comforts I've towld,
  Och, hone! widow Machree,
But you're keeping some poor fellow out in the cowld,
  Och, hone! widow Machree;
    With such sins on your head,
    Shure your pace would be fled,
    Could you slape in your bed
    Without thinking to see
      Some ghost or some sprite
      That would wake you each night—
Crying, och, hone! widow Machree.

Then take my advice, darling widow Machree,
  Och, hone! widow Machree;
And with my advice, faith, I wish you'd take me,
  Och, hone! widow Machree;
    You'd have me to desire,
    Then to stir up the fire,
    And shure hope is no liar
    In whispering to me
      That the ghosts would depart
      When you'd me near your heart;
Och, hone! widow Machree.

Widow Machree, I don't wish to be bold,
  Och, hone! widow Machree;
But with these inducements that I have just told,
  Och, hone! widow Machree,
    I give you my word,
    My own, my adored,
    And as a reward
    Take this promise from me,
      'To atone for my sins
      Your first child shall be twins—
Och, hone! widow Machree.

MOLLY BAWN.

Oh. Molly Bawn, why leave me pining,
  All lonely waiting here for you,
While the stars above are brightly shining,
  Because they've nothing else to do;
The flowers late were open keeping,
  To try a rival blush with you,
But their mother Nature set them sleeping

With their rosy faces washed with dew.
Oh, Molly Bawn, why leave me pining,
All lonely waiting here for you,
The stars above are brightly shining,
Because they've nothing else to do.
Oh! Molly Bawn, Molly Bawn.

Now the pretty flowers were made to bloom, dear,
And the pretty stars were made to shine,
And the pretty girls were made for boys, dear,
And may be you were made to be mine;
The wicked watch-dog here is snarling,
He takes me for a thief you see,
For he knew I'd steal you, Molly, darlin',
And then transported I should be.
Oh, Molly Bawn, why leave me pining,
All lonely waiting here for you,
The stars above are brightly shining,
Because they've nothing else to do.
Oh! Molly Bawn, Molly Bawn.

THE OLD FOLKS ARE GONE.

Far, far in many lands I've wandered
Sadly and alone,
My heart was ever turning Southward
To all the dear ones at home;
Here after all my weary roaming,
At early dawn,
I've come and find the cot still standing,
But, oh, the old folks are gone.
Here I wander sad and lonely,
In the dear old home,
Those that I love so well and fondly
All the old folks are gone.

Here's where I frolick'd with my brother,
Under the tree;
Here's where I knelt beside my mother,
From care and sorrow free;
Still sing the little birds as sweetly,
At night and morn,
Still runs the little brook so fleetly,
But oh, the old folks are gone.
Here I wander sad and lonely,

In the dear old home,
    Those that I love so well and fondly
    All the old folks are gone.

Down where the old banana's waving,
    They're laid to rest,
Where the Swanee's peaceful water's laving
    The green turf o'er their breast;
But there's a home I know where parting
    Never can come;
Oh, for that home I must be starting,
    There's where the old folks are gone.
    Here I wander sad and lonely,
        In the dear old home,
    Those that I love so well and fondly
        All the old folks are gone.

——————

ANNIE BELL.

We stood upon the balcony,
    Sweet Annie Bell and I,
To trace once more the Southern Cross,*
    Then radiant in the sky;
Our thoughts were sad, and sad my heart,
    While tears bedim'd her eye,
For we were soon to part 'or aye,
    Sweet Annie Bell and I.
Sweet Annie Bell! dear Annie Bell!
    For we were soon to part for aye,
    Sweet Annie Bell and I.

I saw her gentle bosom heave,
    With deep emotions stirred;
And closer press'd her hand in mine,
    But utter'd not a word.
Dear Annie Bell! what anguish wrung
    That spotless heart of thine!
Yet ah! the beating of that heart
    Could not compare with mine.
Sweet Annie Bell! dear Annie Bell!
    For we were soon to part for aye,
    Sweet Annie Bell and I.

——————
*A phenomenon peculiar to Southern latitudes—the appearance
of a cross in the heavens.

The hopes which made life beautiful,
  And strew'd my path with flowers,
Were center'd in that lovely form,
  Dear Annie Bell, of you s;
And now how dark and desolate
  The rolling years pass by,;
Alone I gaze upon th cross,
  Still radiant in the sky.
Sweet Annie Bell! dear Annie Bell!
  For we were soon to part for aye,
  Sweet Annie Bell and I.

— — —

FAIRY DELL.

Wilt thou meet me in the Fairy Dell, love,
  When twilight draweth near;
And I'll whisper what I have to tell, love,
  Softly in thine ear:
We will rove where fairies nightly trip, love,
  When mortal steps be gone,
And the cup of happiness we'll sip, love,
  Ere night's shade comes on.
    Then meet me here at twilight,
      For I've something sweet to tell,
    And you'll hear it with more true delight,
      If told in Fairy Dell.

Soon the twilight hour will be past, love,
  That hour dear to me,
When all sorrow far behind I cast, love,
  As I fly to thee.
Hasten quickly ere the coming night, love,
  My fondest hopes dispel,
Ere the joyous dreams I've formed take flight, love,
  Haste to Fairy Dell.
    Then meet me here at twilight,
      For I've something sweet to tell,
    And you'll hear it with more true delight,
      If told in Fairy Dell.

I am weary waiting all alone, love,
  I'd ever be with thee,
Could I hear once more thy gentle tone, love,
  Ah! what joy to me;
For my heart is so entwined with thee, love,

It lives but where thou art,
Oh! come tell me that thou wilt be mine, love,
Never more to part.
Then meet me here at twilight,
For I've something sweet to tell,
And you'll hear it with more true delight,
If told in Fairy Dell.

POOR JACK.

Go patter to lubbers and swabs, do ye see,
'Bout danger, and fear and the like;
A tight water-boat and good sea room give me,
And it aint to a little I'll strike;
Though the tempest top-gallant masts smack-smooth should smite,
And shiver each splinter of wood,
Clear the wreck, stow the yards, and bouse everything tight,
And under reef'd foresail we'll scud;
Avast! nor don't think me a milksop so soft,
To be taken for trifles aback,
For they say there's a Providence sits up aloft,
To keep watch for the life of poor Jack!

I heard our good Chaplain palaver one day
About souls, heaven, mercy and such;
And, my timbers! what lingo he'd coil and belay,
Why, 'twas just all as one as High Dutch;
For he said, how a sparrow can't flounder, d'ye see,
Without orders that come down below,
And many fine things, that proved clearly to me
That Providence takes us in tow;
For, says he, do you mind me, let storms e'er so oft
Take the top-sails of sailors aback.
There's a sweet little Cherub that sits up aloft
To keep watch for the life of poor Jack!

I said to our Poll, for d'ye see, she would cry,
When last we weighed anchor for sea,
What argufies sniv'ling and piping your eye?
Why, what a d——d fool you must be!
Can't you see, the world's wide, and there's room for us all,
Both for seamen and lubbers ashore?
And if to old Davy I should go, friend Poll,
You never will hear of me more;
What then? all's a hazard; come don't be so soft;

Perhaps I may laughing come back.
For, d'ye see, there's a Cherub sits smiling aloft,
To keep watch for the life of poor Jack?

D'ye mind me, a sailor should be every inch,
All as one as a piece of the ship,
And with her brave the world without offering to flinch,
From the moment the anchor's a trip
As for one, in all weathers, all times, sides and ends,
Naught's a trouble from duty that springs,
For my heart is my Poll's, and my rhino's my friend's,
And as for my life, 'tis the king's;
Even when my time comes, ne'er believe me so soft
As for grief to be taken aback,
For the same little Cherub that sits up aloft
Will look out a good berth for poor Jack!

EXILE OF ERIN.

There came to the beach a poor exile of Erin,
The dew on his thin robe was heavy and chill.
For his country he sigh'd, when at twilight repairing,
To wander alone by the wind-beaten hill.
But the day-star attracted his eye's sad devotion,
For it rose o'er his own native isle of the ocean,
Where once, in the glow of his youthful emotion,
He sang the bold anthem of Erin Go Bragh.

O, sad is my fate! said the heart-broken stranger,
The wild deer and wolf to a covert can flee,
But I have no refuge from famine and danger,
A home and a country remain not to me;
Ah! never again in the green shady bowers,
Where my forefathers lived shall I spend the sweet hours;
Or cover my heart with the wild woven flowers
Or strike to the numbers of Erin Go Bragh.

O, where is the cottage that stood by the wild wood,
Sisters and sire, did ye weep for its fall!
O, where is my mother, that watched o'er my childhood,
And where is the bosom friend dearer than all!
Ah, my sad soul long abandon'd by pleasure,
O, why did it doat on a fast fading treasure:
Years like the rain drops may fall without measure,
But rapture and beauty they cannot recall!

Erin, my country, though sad and forsaken,
In dreams I revisit thy sea-beaten shore;
But alas! in a far distant land I awaken,
And sigh for the friends who can meet no more!
O, hard, cruel fate, wilt thou never replace me,
In a mansion of peace, where no peril can chase me!
Ah, never again shall my brothers embrace me,
They died to defend me, or lived to deplore.

But yet, all its fond recollection suppressing,
One dying wish my lone bosom shall draw,
Erin, an exile bequeaths thee his blessing,
Land of my forefathers, Erin Go Bragh.
Burie and cold, while my heart stills its emotion,
Green be thy fields, sweetest isle of the ocean,
And thy harp striking bards sing aloud with devotion,
O, Erin Ma Vourneen, Erin Go Bragh!

MYNHEER VON DUNCK.

Mynheer Von Dunck,
Though he never got drunk,
Sipped brandy and water daily;
And he quenched his thirst
With two quarts of the first,
To a pint of the latter daily,
Singing, "Oh that a Dutchman's draught might be
As deep as the rolling Zuyder Zee!"

Water well mingled with spirit good store,
No Hollander dreams of scorning;
But of water alone he drinks no more
Than a rose supplies
When a dew-drop lies
On its bloom of a summer morning.

LOVE NOT.

Love not! love not! ye hapless sons of clay;
Hope's gayest wreath are made of earthly flowers,
Things that are made to fade and fall away,
Ere they have blossomed for a few short hours.
Love not! Love not!

Love not! love not! the things you love may die,
  May perish from the gay and gladsome earth;
The silent stars, the blue and smiling sky,
  Beams on its grave as once upon its birth.
      Love not! love not!

Love not! love not! the thing you love may change;
  The rosy lip may cease to smile on you,
The kindly beaming eye grow cold and strange,
  The heart still warmly beat, yet not be true.
      Love not! love not!

Love not! love not! oh, warning vainly said—
  In present hours, as in years gone by,
Love flings a halo round the dear one's head,
  Faultless, immortal, till they change or die.
      Love not! love not!

THOU ART GONE.

Thou art gone, but I am keeping
  In my heart thy treasur'd name,
If I'm smiling, if I'm weeping,
  Thou art with me all the same.
Yes, the link at last is riven,
  All our pleasant dreams are o'er,
And, unless we meet in heaven,
  Thou wilt never see me more.
Thou art gone, but I am keeping
  In my heart thy treasur'd name,
If I'm smiling, if I'm weeping,
  Thou art with me,
Thou art with me all the same.

JOHNNY WITH A RANGO HI!

In old Virginny State, on massa's old plantation,
      Johnny with a rango hi!
There's niggers by the score all from the color'd nation,
      Johnny with a rango hi!
Sing, sing, darkeys sing, let the fiddle and banjo ring;
Sing, sing, darkeys sing, Johnny with a rango hi!

Sometimes we kill a hog and cut him up on Sunday,
    Johnny with a rango hi!
And when we make a meal there's nothing left for Monday,
    Johnny with a rango hi!
Sing, sing, darkeys sing, let the fiddle and banjo ring;
Sing, sing, darkeys sing, Johnny with a rango hi!

We dive in the corn-cake what's baked in the ashes,
    Johnny with a rango hi!
And old mud-turtles too, what's caught about the mashes,
    Johnny with a rango hi!
Sing, sing, darkeys sing, let the fiddle and banjo ring;
Sing, sing, darkeys sing, Johnny with a rango hi!

When we are dry we take a gourd or two of whiskey,
    Johnny with a rango hi!
And that you know is just what makes a nigger frisky,
    Johnny with a rango hi!
Sing, sing, darkeys sing, let the fiddle and the banjo ring;
Sing, sing, darkeys sing, Johnny with a rango hi!

Oh, have you never seen the gal that wears a josey,
    Johnny with a rango hi!
The colored poet say that she's the Southern posey,
    Johnny with a rango hi!
Sing, sing, darkeys sing, let the fiddle and banjo ring;
Sing, sing, darkeys sing, Johnny with a rango hi!

She's scratched into my heart and there she's made her quarters,
    Johnny with a rango hi!
For she's the greatest swell of all Virginny's daughters,
    Johnny with a rango hi!
Sing, sing, darkeys sing, let the fiddle and banjo ring;
Sing, sing, darkeys sing, Johnny with a rango hi!

HOOP DE DOODEN DO.

Susy in de kitchen, hoop de dooden do,
Susy in de kitchen, hoop de dooden do;
Susy in de kitchen shelling out the peas,
Master in the parlor tasting of the cheese.
What's the matter, Susy, what's the matter my dear,
What's the matter, Susy, O, I'm going to leave you now;
Play upon the fiddle, come play upon the drum,
Play upon the banjo, Susy can't you come.

The big dog he bow-wow, hoop de dooden do,
The big dog he bow-wow. hoop de dooden do;
The big dog he bow-wow watching at the gate,
He smell the meat a trying and then he could'nt wait.
Then what's the matter, Susy. what's the matter my dear,
What's the matter, Sosy, O, I'm going to leave you now;
Come play upon the fiddle, play upon the drum,
Play upon the banjo, Susy can't you come.

The old horse he kick high, hoop de dooden do,
The old horse he kick high, hoop de dooden do;
The old horse he kick high, standing in the stable,
Old master try to ketch him, but found he wa 'nt able.
Then what's the matter, Susy, what's the matter my dear,
What's the matter, Susy, O, I'm going to leave you now;
Come play upon the fiddle. play upon the drum,
Play upon the banj', Susy can't you come.

The hen flew in the garden, hoop de dooden do,
The hen flew in the garden, hoop ne dooden do;
The hen flew in the garden, Master try to ketch him,
He fell against the lamp-post, and then he did'nt fetch him;
Then what's the matter, Susy, what's the matter my dear,
What's the matter, Susy, O, I'm going to leave you now;
Come play upon the fiddle play upon the drum,
Play upon the banjo, Susy can't you come.

BESSY, THE SAILOR'S BRIDE.

Poor Bessy, was a sailor's bride,
    And he was off to sea,
Their only child was by their side,
    And who so sad as she?

Forget me not, forget me not,
    When you are far from me,
And whatsoe'er poor Bessy's lot,
    She will remember thee.

A twelve month scarce had passed away,
    As it was told to me,
When Willy with a gladsome heart,
    Came home again from sea.

He bounded up the craggy path,
 And sought his cottage door,
But his poor wife and lovely child,
 Poor Willy saw no more.

"Forget me not, forget me not,"
 The words rung in his ear,
He asked his neighbors one by one,
 Each answer'd with a tear.

They pointed to the old church-yard—
 And there his youthful bride,
With the pretty child they loved so well,
 Were resting side by side.

POPE AND SULTAN.

The Pope lives glorious in the land,
 Ablution fees are e'er at hand;
He drinks the very best of wine,
 I wish the Pope's estate were mine.

But no, he is a sorry wight;
 He tastes not love's supreme delight;
No maiden's arms to him are ope—
 No, no, I would not be the Pope.

The Sultan lives in mighty state,
 He has a palace wide and great;
With many a wife with pretty face;
 I wish mine were the Sultan's place.

And yet I've pity on the man;
 If he obeys his Alkoran,
He canno drink one drop of wine—
 No, no, this were no choice of mine.

Alone, with neither would I change,
 Not for a moment's speedy range;
Yet cheerfully would I agree
 To bear by turns each dignity,

Therefore, sweet love, one kiss from thee,
For now the Sultan I will be;
Now, brothers, fill with sparkling wine,
For now the Pope's estate is mine.

JUANITA.

Soft o'er the fountain
  Lingering falls the Southern moon;
Far o'er the mountain
  Breaks the day too soon!
In thy dark eye's splendor,
  Where the warm light loves to dwell,
Weary looks, yet tender,
  Speak their fond farewell!
Nita! Juanita!
  Ask thy soul if we should part!
Nita! Juanita!
Lean thou on my heart.

When in thy dreaming
  Moons like these shall shine again,
And day-light beaming
  Prove thy dreams are vain.
Wilt thou not, relenting,
  For thine absent lover sigh,
In thy heart consenting
  To a prayer gone by?
Nita! Juanita!
Let me linger by thy side!
Nita! Juanita!
Be my own fair bride!

THE LASS THAT LOVES A SAILOR.

The moon on the ocean was dimm'd by a ripple,
  Affording a chequered light,
The gay jolly tars passed the word for a tipple,
  And the toast, for 'twas Saturday night.
    Some sweetheart or wife,
    He loved as his life,
Each drank, and he wish'd he could hail her;
  But the standing toast

That pleased the most,
Was the wind that blows,
The ship that goes,
And the lass that loves a sailor.

Some drank his country, and some her brave ships,
    And some the Constitution,
Some, may the Yanks, and all such rips,
    Yield to Southern resolution,
        That fate might bless
        Some Poll or Bess,
And that they soon might hail her.
        But the standing toast
        That pleased the most,
        Was the wind that blows,
        The ship that goes,
And the lass that loves a sailor.

Some drank the navy and some our land,
    This glorious land of freedom;
Some that our tars may never want
    Heroes brave to lead them,
That she who's in distress may find
    Such friends that ne'er will fail her;
        But the standing toast
        That pleased the most,
        Was the wind that blows,
        The ship that goes,
And the lass that loves a sailor.

KATHLEEN MAVOURNEEN.

Kathleen Mavourneen, the grey dawn is breaking,
    The horn of the hunter is heard on the hill,
The lark from her light wing the bright dew drop is shaking,
    Kathleen Mavourneen, what, slumbering still?

Oh! hast thou forgotten how soon we must sever,
    Oh! hast thou forgotten, this day we must part?
It may be for years, and it may be forever;
    Oh! why art thou silent, thou voice of my heart?

Kathleen Mavourneen, oh! wake from thy slumber,
    The blue mountains glow in the sun's golden light;
Oh! where is the spell that once hung on thy slumbers?
    Arise in thy beauty, thou star of the night!
                    Kathleen, &c.

THE LOW-BACKED CAR.

When first I saw sweet Peggy,
  'Twas on a market day,
On a low backed car she drove, and sat
  Upon a truss of hay.
But when that hay was blooming grass,
  And decked with flowers of spring;
No flowers were there that could compare
  With the lovely girl I sing.
As she sat in her low-backed car,
The man at the turnpike bar
  Never asked for his toll,
  But just rubbed his old poll,
And looked after the low-backed car.

In battle's wild commotion,
  The proud and mighty Mars,
In hostile scythes demands his tithes
  Of death in warlike scars.
But Peggy, peaceful goddess,
  Has darts in her bright eye
That knocks men down in the market town,
  As right and left they fly;
As she sits in her low-backed car,
They are hit from her near and afar,
  And the doctor's art
  Cannot cure the smart
That is hit from the low-backed car.

That Peggy round her car, sirs,
  Has strings of ducks and geese,
But the scores of hearts she slaughters
  By far outnumber these;
While she among her poultry sits,
  Just like a turtle dove,
Well worth the cage, I do engage,
  Of the blooming god of love.
As she sat in her low-backed car,
Her lovers come near and far,
  And annoy the chicken
  That Peggy is picking,
As she sits in her low-backed car.

I'd rather own that car, sirs,
  With Peggy by my side,
Than a coach and four and gold galore
  And a lady for my bride;

For the lady would sit *foreninst* me,
  On a cushion made with taste,
But Peggy would sit beside me
  With my arm around her waist.
As we drove in the low-backed car
To be married by Father Maher,
  Oh my heart would beat high,
    At her glance or her sigh,
Tho' it beat in a low-backed car.

NERVOUS FAMILY.

Air—" We're all Noddin."

We're all nervous, shake, shake, trembling,
We're all nervous, at our house, at home,
There's myself and my mother, my sister and brother,
If left all alone, are frightened at each other.
Our dog was away if a stranger's in the house,
And our tabby cat, too, is frightened at a mouse;
And we are all nervous, shake, shake, trembling;
We're all nervous at our house, at home.

We all at dinner, shake, shake, at carving;
And as for snuffing, we oft snuff out the light.
Last night every one did to snuff the candle try,
But my wife could'nt do it, nor my sister nor could I.
Come give me the snuffers, said mother, with a flout,
I'll show you how to do it, and she snuff'd the candle out.
For she's so nervous, shake, shake trembling,
We're all nervous at our house, at home.

My nervous wife can't work at her needle,
And my shaking hand spills half my cup of tea;
When wine at dinner my timid sister's taking
It's spilt on the table, for so her hand is shaking.
My mother taking snuff, very carefully doth try
To pop it up her nose, when she pops it in her eye.
For she is so nervous, shake, shake, trembling;
We're all nervous at our house, at home.

Our nerves foretell all the changes of the weather;
We are so nervous we're frightened at each noise;
We have got a private watchman to guard the private door,
But since we have had him, we are frightened more and more,

For he falls asleep, and we've found out too that he,
In respect to his nerves, oh, he's quite as bad as we.
And we're all nervous, shake, shake, trembling;
We're all nervous at our house, at home.

ROSALIE, THE PRAIRIE FLOWER.

On the distant prairie, where the heather wild
In its quiet beauty lived and smil'd,
Stands a little cottage, and a creeping vine
Loves around its porch to twine;
In that peaceful dwelling was a lovely child,
With her blue eyes beaming, soft and mild,
And the wavy ringlets of the flaxen hair
Floating in the summer air.
    Fair as a lily, joyous and free,
    Light of that prairie home was she,
Every one who knew her, felt the gentle power
Of Rosalie, the prairie flower.

On the distant prairie, when the days were long,
Tripping like a fairy, sweet her song,
With the sunny blossoms and the birds at play,
Beautiful and bright as they;
When twilight's shadows gathered in the west,
And the voice of nature sunk to rest,
Like a cherub kneeling seemed the lovely child,
With her gentle eyes so mild.

But the summer faded, and a chilly blast
O'er that happy cottage swept at last,
When autumn song-birds woke the dewy morn,
Little prairie flower was gone;
For the angels whispered softly in her ear,
"Child, thy father calls thee, stay not here;"
And gently bore her, robed in spotless white,
To their blissful home of light.

SOLDIER'S DREAM.

Our bugles sang truce, for the night cloud had lower'd
  And the sentinel stars set their watch in the sky,
And thousands had sunk on the ground overpowered,
  The weary to sleep and the wounded to die.

3

When reposing that night on a pallet of straw,
  By the wolf-scaring fagot that guarded the slain,
At the dead of the night a sweet vision I saw,
  And thrice ere the morning I dream'd it again.

Methought from the battle-field's dreadful array,
  Far I had roamed on a desolate track,
'Twas autumn—and sunshine arose on the way,
  To the home of my father that welcom'd me back.

I flew to the pleasant field travelled so oft,
  In life's morning march when my bosom was young,
I heard my own mountain goats bleating aloft,
  And knew the sweet strain that the corn reapers sung.

Then pledg'd we the wine cup, and fondly I swore,
  From my home and my weeping friends never to part,
My little ones kiss'd me a thousand times o'er,
  And my wife sobb'd aloud in the fullness of heart.

Stay, stay with us—rest, thou art weary and worn,
  And fain was the war-worn soldier to stay,
But sorrow returned with the dawning of morn,
  And the voice of my dreaming ear melted away.

NORA McCARTY.

Nora is pretty,
Nora is witty,
Witty and pretty as pretty can be !
She's the completest
Of girls and the neatest,
The brightest and sweetest,
But she's not for me !
Mavourneen.

Nora, be still, you,
Nora why will you,
Be witty and pretty as pretty can be—
So strong and so slender,
So haughty and tender,
So sweet in your splendor—
And yet not for me ?
Mavourneen.

LORENA.

The years creep slowly by, Lorena,
The snow is on the grass again,
The Sun's low down the sky, Lorena,
The frost gleams where the flowers have been,
But the heart throbs on as warmly now,
As when the summer days were nigh,
Oh! the Sun can never dip so low
Adown affection's cloudless sky!

A hundred months have passed, Lorena,
Since last I held that hand in mine,
And felt the pulse beat fast, Lorena,
Though mine beat faster far than thine;
A hundred months, 'twas flowry May,
When up the hilly slope we climbed,
To watch the dying of the day,
And hear the distant church-bells chime.

We loved each other then, Lorena,
More than we ever cared to tell,
And what we might have been, Lorena,
Had but our loving prospered well;
But then 'tis past, the years are gone,
I'll not call up their shadowy forms,
I'll say to them lost years sleep on,
Sleep on, nor heed life's pelting storm.

The story of the past, Lorena,
Alas! care not to repeat,
The hopes that could not last, Lorena,
They lived but only lived to cheat;
I would not cause even one regret
To rankle in your bosom now,
For if we try we may forget,
Were words of thine long years ago.

Yes these were words of thine, Lorena,
They burn within my memory yet,
They touched some tender chords, Lorena,
That thrill and tremble with regret;
'Twas not thy woman's heart that spoke,
Thy heart was always true to me,
A duty stern and pressing broke
The tie which linked my soul to thine.

It matters little now, Lorena,
The past is in the eternal past,
Our heads will soon lie low, Lorena,
Life's tide is ebbing out so fast;
There is a future oh! thank God!
Of life this is so small a part,
'Tis dust to dust beneath the sod,
But there, up there, 'tis heart to heart.

A THOUSAND A YEAR.

ROBIN RUFF—

If I had but a thousand a year, Gaffer Green—
If I had but a thousand a year,
What a man would I be, and what sights would I see,
If I had but a thousand a year.

GAFFER GREEN—

The best wish you could have, take my word, Robin Ruff,
Would scarce find you in bread or in beer;
But be honest and true, say what would you do,
If you had but a thousand a year.

ROBIN RUFF—

I'd do—I scarcely know what, Gaffer Green,
I'd go—faith, I scarcely know where;
I'd scatter the chink, and leave others to think,
If I had but a thousand a year.

GAFFER GREEN—

But when you are aged and gray, Robin Ruff,
And the day of your death it draws near,
Say, what with your pains, would you do with your gains
If you then had a thousand a year?

ROBIN RUFF—

I scarcely can tell what you mean, Gaffer Green,
For your questions are always so queer;
But as other folks die, I suppose so must I—

GAFFER GREEN,

What! and give up your thousand a year?

There's a place that is better than this, Robin Ruff—
And I hope in my heart you'll go there—
Where the poor man's as great though he hath no estate,
Ay, as if he'd a thousand a year.

I'M A PILGRIM.

I'm a pilgrim, and I'm a stranger,
I can tarry, I can tarry but a night;
I'm a pilgrim, and I'm a stranger,
I can tarry, I can tarry but a night.
  Do not detain me, for I am going
  Where the streamlets are ever flowing;
I'm a pilgrim, and I'm a stranger,
I can tarry, I can tarry but a night.

Where the sunbeams are ever shining,
I am longing, I am longing for the sight,
  Within a country unknown and dreary
  I have been wand'ring, forlorn and weary.
I'm a pilgrim, and I'm a stranger,
I can tarry, I can tarry but a night.

Of that country to which I'm going,
My Redeemer, my Redeemer is the light,
  There's no sorrow, nor any sighing,
  Nor any sin there, nor any dying.
I'm a pilgrim, and I'm a stranger,
I can tarry, I can tarry but a night.

I'VE LOVED THEE LONG.

I know that thou hast many friends,
  And some who love thee well;
But none like me have ever bowed
  Before thy beauty's spell.
I've loved thee as the wild flow'rs love
  The sun at morn's first hour,
Or as the parch'd and thirsty earth
  Doth love the cooling shower.
My life has been a dream of love,
  Its dearest idol thou ;
That love is faithful still to thee ;
  Then why this coldness now ?

I've loved thee long ; through grief and pain
  Thy image still was dear ;
But thou hast scorned my honest love,
  And caused me many a tear.
Yet, should hope's star grow dim to thee,
  And friends in coldness turn,

My love would then more warmly glow,
　Its flame more brightly burn;
I'd never give thy heart one pang
　By friendship's broken vow,
Or bid thee e'er distrust my love;
　Then why this coldness now?

No, not like thee would I have turned;
　Should all from thee depart,
With words of love and hope I'd draw
　Thee closer to my heart;
And should thy summer friends forsake
　One they profess'd to love,
My heart should prove a shelt'ring ark
　To the poor homeless dove;
Should e'er life's storm thy bark assail,
　And waves dash o'er its prow,
I'd still be near to share thy fate;
　Then why this coldness now?

I SHOULD LIKE TO MARRY.

Oh! I should like to marry,
　If I could but find
Some young and handsome fellow
　Suited to my mind;
Oh! I should like him dashing,
　Oh! I should like him gay,
The leader of the fashion
　And dandy of the day;
Oh! I should like to marry,
　If I could but find
Some young and dashing fellow
　Suited to my mind.

Oh! I should like to marry,
　For I'm sore afraid
That, if I longer tarry,
　I'll die a lone old maid.
Oh! I should like him witty,
　And I should like him good,
And with a little money—
　Yes, indeed! I should.
Oh! I should like to marry,
　If I could but find
Some young and dashing fellow
　Suited to my mind.

Oh! I should like him pretty,
  And let his feet be small;
'And then, to make him noble,
  I'd have him rather tall.
Oh! let his form be upright,
  Both elegant and free,
And if his eyes are only black
  I'm sure we can agree.
Oh! I should like t marry,
  If I could but find
Some young and dashing fellow
  Suited to my mind.

Oh! I should like him handsome,
  That he might cut a dash;
A stout and noble figure,
  With wh.skers and moustache.
His hair, I'd like it curly,
  And o'er his brow to fall;
I'd always dress him showy,
  And have him wear a shawl.
Oh! I should like to marry,
  If I could but find
Some young and handsome fellow
  Suited to my mind.

KITTY TYRRELL.

You're looking as fresh as the morn, darling,
  You're looking as bright as the day;
But while on your charms I'm dilating,
  You're stealing my poor heart away;
But keep it, and welcome, Mavourneen,
  It's loss I'm not going to mourn;
Yet one heart's enough for a body,
  So pray give me your's in return—
    Mavourneen, Mavourneen,
      So pray give me your's in return.

I've built me a neat little cot, darling,
  I've pigs and potatoes in store,
I've twenty good pounds in the bank, love,
  And maybe a pound or two more;
It's all very well to have riches,
  But I'm such a covetous elf,

I can't help still sighing for something,
  And darling, that something's yourself—
    Mavourneen, Mavourneen,
      That something, you know, is yourself.

You're smiling, and that's a good sign, darling,
  Say yes, and you'll never repent,
Or if you would rather be silent,
  Your silence I'll take for consent;
That good-natured dimple's a telltale,
  Now all that I have is your own;
This week you may be Kitty Tyrrell,
  Next week you'll be Kitty Malone—
    Mavourneen, Mavourneen,
      You'll be my own Mistress Malone.

FAIRY BOY.

A mother came, when stars were paling,
  Wailing round a lonely spring;
Thus she cried, while tears were falling,
  Calling on the Fairy King:
Why with spells my child caressing,
  Courting him with fairy joy?
Why destroy a mother's blessing?
  Wherefore steal my baby boy?

O'er the mountain, through the wildwood,
  Where his childhood loved to play,
Where the flow'rs are freshly springing,
  There I wander day by day;
There I wander, growing fonder
  Of the child that made my joy,
On the echoes wildly calling
  To restore my fairy boy.

But in vain my plaintive calling;
  Tears are falling all in vain;
He now sports with fairy pleasure,
  He's the treasure of their train.
Fare thee well, my child, forever;
  In this world I've lost my joy;
But in the next we ne'er shall sever—
  There I'll find my angel boy.

CHARGE OF THE LIGHT BRIGADE.

Half a league, half a league,
  Half a league onward,
All in the valley of death
  Rode the six hundred.
Theirs not to reason why,
Theirs not to make reply,
Theirs but to do and die—
Into the valley of death
  Rode the six hundred.

Cannon to right of them,
Cannon to left of them,
Cannon in front of them
  Volley'd and thunder'd,
Stormed at with shot and shell,
Boldly they rode and well;
Into the jaws of death,
Into the mouth of hell,
    Rode the six hundred.

Flash'd all their sabres bare,
Flash'd all at once in air,
Sab'ring the gunners there,
Charging an army, while
  All the world wonder'd;
Plunged in the battery smoke,
Fiercely the line they broke;
Strong was the sabre-stroke—
Making an army reel
  Shaken and sunder'd.
Then they rode back, but not,
  Not the six hundred.

Cannon to right of them,
Cannon to left of them,
Cannon behind them,
  Volley'd and thunder'd
Stormed at with shot and shell,
They that had struck so well,
Rode through the jaws of death,
Half a league back again,
Up from the mouth of hell,
All that was left of them,
  Left of six hundred.
Honor the brave and bold!

Long shall the tale be told,
Yea, when our babe's are old,
How they rode onward!

KNIGHT AND LADY.

A Knight and a lady once met in a grove,
While each was in quest of a fugitive love,
A river ran mournfully murmuring by,
And they wept in its waters for sympathy.

Oh, never was knight such a sorrow that bore,
Oh, never was maid so deserted before!
"From life and its woes let us instantly fly,
And jump in together for company!"

They searched for an ed y that suited the deed,
But here was a bramble and there was a weed,
"How tiresome it is!" said the fair with a sigh,
So they sat down to rest them in company.

They gazed on each other, the maid and the knight—
How fair was her form, and how goodly his height—
"One mournful embrace," sobbed the youth, "ere I die!"
So kissing and crying kept company.

"Oh, had I but loved such an angel as you!"
"Oh, had but my swain been a quarter as true!"
"To miss such perfection how blind was I!"
Sure now they were excellent company!

At length spoke the lass, 'twixt a smile and a tear,
"The weather is cold for a watery bier,
When summer returns we may easily die,
Till then let us sorrow in company!"

BURIAL OF SIR JOHN MOORE.

Not a drum was heard, nor a funeral note,
As his c rse to the ramparts we buried,
Not a soldier discharged his farewell shot

O'er the grave where our hero was buried,
We buried him darkly, at dead of night,
The turf with our bayonets turning.
By the struggling moonbeam's misty light,
And our lanterns dimly burning.

Few and short were the prayers we said,
And we spoke not a word of sorrow,
But we steadfastly gazed on the face of the dead,
And we bitterly thought of the morrow.
No useless coffin confined his breast,
Nor in sheet, nor in shroud, we bound him;
But he lay, like a warrior taking his rest,
With his martial cloak around him.

We thought, as we hollowed his narrow bed,
And smooth'd down his lonely pillow,
That the foe and the stranger would tread o'er his head,
And we far away on the billow,
Lightly they'll talk of the spirit that's gone,
And o'er his cold ashes upbraid him;
But nothing he'll reck if they let him sleep on
In the grave where a Briton has laid him.

But half our heavy task was done
When the clock told the hour for retiring,
And we heard by the distant and random gun
That the foe was suddenly firing.
Slowly and sadly we laid him down,
From the field of his fame, fresh and gory—
We carv'd not a line, we rais'd not a stone,
But we left him alone in his glory.

SERENADE.

Slumber, gentle lady,
Slumber like the rose
When the air of heaven
Lulls thee to repose.

Angels hover o'er thee,
Softly seal thine eyes,
Waft thy spirit lightly
To the smiling skies.

ANGEL'S WHISPER.

A baby was sleeping,
Its mother was weeping,
For her husband was far o'er the wide raging sea,
And the tempest was swelling
Round the fisherman's dwelling,
And she cried " Dermot, darling, oh come back to me.'

Her beads while she numbered,
The baby still slumbered,
And smiled in her face as she bended her knee;
Oh! blest be that warning
My child's sleep adorning,
For I know that the angels are whispering to thee.

And while they are keeping
Bright watch o'er thy sleeping,
Ah, pray to them softly, my baby, with me;
And say thou would'st rather
They'd watch o'er thy father,
For I know that the angels are whispering to thee.

The dawn of the morning
Saw Dermot returning,
And the wife wept with joy the babe's father to see,
And closely caressing
The child with a blessing,
Said, I knew that the angels were whispering to thee.

ONE LOOK OF LOVE.

One look of love from those bright eyes,
To cheer this anxious breast—
One smile from thee I'd fondly prize,
And be forever blest;
Will not my sighs to pity move thee—
Say, say thou'lt be mine,
And bless the heart that fondly loves thee;
Then turn not from me, maiden fair,
Nor bid me plead in vain
For one kind look my heart to cheer,
One smile to soothe my pain.

SOLDIER'S WISH.

It is not on the battle-field that I would wish to die,
It is not on the broken shield I'd breathe my latest sigh,
And though a soldier knows not how to dread a soldier's doom,
I ask no laurel for my brow, no trophy for my tomb.

It is not that I scorn the wreath a soldier proudly wears;
It is not that I fear the death a soldier proudly dares;
When slaughtered comrades round me lie, I'd be the last to
    yield,
But—yet I do not wish to die upon the battle-field.

When faint and bleeding in the fray, oh! let me then retain
Enough of life to crawl away to this sweet vale again;
For like the wounded, weary dove that flutters o'er its nest,
I fain would reach my own dear love, and die upon her breast.

WHAT FAIRY-LIKE MUSIC.

What fairy-like music steals over the sea,
Entrancing the senses with charm'd melody?
'Tis the voice of the mermaid that floats o'er the main,
As she mingles her song with the gondolier's strain!

The winds are all hush'd, and the water's at rest,
They sleep like the passions in infancy's breast,
'Till storms shall unchain them from out their dark cave,
And break the repose of the soul and the wave.

CORPORAL CASEY.

When I was at home I was merry and frisky,
My dad kept a pig and my mother sold whiskey,
My uncle was rich, but would never be aisy,
Till I was enlisted by Corporal Casey;
Och! rub-a-dub, row-de-dow, Corporal Casey.
My dear little Shelah I thought would run crazy
When I trudged away with tough Corporal Casey.

I march'd from Kilkenny, and as I was thinking
On Shelah, my heart in my bosom was sinking,

But soon I was forced to look fresh as a daisy,
For fear of a drubbing from Corporal Casey.
Och! rub-a-dub, row-de-dow, Corporal Casey!
The devil go with him! I ne'er could be lazy,
He stuck in my skirts so, old Corporal Casey.

We went into battle, I took the blows fairly,
They fell on my pate, but they bother'd me rarely,
And who sh uld the first be that drop't? why so plase ye,
It was my good friend, honest Corporal Casey;
Och! rub-a-drub, row-de.dow, Corporal Casey!
Think's I, you are quiet, and I shall be aisy;
So eight years I fought without Corporal Casey.

KITTY OF COLERAINE.

As beautiful Kitty one morning was tripping,
    With a pitcher of milk from the fair of Coleraine,
When she saw me she stumbl'd, the pitcher it tumbl'd,
    And all the sweet buttermilk water'd the plain;
Oh! what shall I do now, twas looking at you now,
    Sure, sure, such a pitcher I'll ne er meet again;
'Twas the pride of my dairy—O! Barney McCleary,
    You're sent as a plague to the girls of Coleraine.

I sat down beside her and gently did chide her,
    That such a misfortune should give her such pain,
A kiss then I gave her, and, before I did lave her,
    She vow'd for such pleasure she'd break it again.
'Twas hay-making season, I can't tell you the reason,
    Misfortune will never come single, 'tis plain,
For, very soon after poor Kitty's disaster,
    The devil a pitcher was whole in Coleraine!

AUNT JEMIMA'S PLASTER.

Aunt Jemima, she was old,
    But very kind and clever;
She had a notion of her own
    That she would marry never.
She said that she would live in peace,
    And she would be her master;

She made her living day by day
By selling of a plaster.
Sheepskin and beeswax
Make this awful plaster;
The more you try to take it off,
The more it sticks the faster.

She had a sister, very tall,
And if she'd kept on growing,
She might have been a giant now,
In fact there is no knowing;
All of a sudden she became
Of her own height the master,
And all because upon each foot
Jemima put a plaster.
Sheepskin and beeswax
Make this awful plaster;
The more you try to take it off,
The more it sticks the faster.

Her neighbor had a Thomas cat
That eat like any glutton;
It never caught a mouse or rat,
But stole both milk and mutton;
To keep it home she tried her best,
But ne'er could be its master,
Until she stuck it to the floor
With Aunt Jemima's plaster.
Sheepskin and beeswax
Make this awful plaster;
The more you try to take it off,
The more it sticks the faster.

Now if you have a dog or cat,
A husband, wife, or lover,
That you would wish to keep at home,
This plaster just discover;
And if you wish to live in peace,
Avoiding all disaster,
Take my advice, and try the strength
Of Aunt Jemima's plaster.
Sheepskin and beeswax
Make this awful plaster;
The more you try to take it off,
The more it sticks the faster.

THE FROGS' CONCERT.

Kung de nung—kung, tung,
  Koo te kung, tee koo;
Titteri, titteri kung,
  Titteri, titteri koo!

FULL CHORUS.

Bung de kung—kicka ku,
Te te we, noun de ku.

SOLO SOPRANO.

Tiddery pe de we de kung,
Pee de weet! Pee de weet!

CHORUS OF BASS VOICES.

Kung, kung, trata kung,
Diggory kum, te kum te boo.

TREE-TOAD SOLO.

Tr—a—a ta weet!
Weeterry dee!

ELLEN BAYNE.

Soft be thy slumbers!
  Rude cares, depart!
Visions in numbers
  Cheer thy young heart!
Dream on while bright hours
  And fond hopes remain,
Blooming, like smiling flowers,
  For thee, Ellen Bayne!
Gentle slumbers o'er thee glide,
Dreams of beauty round thee bide,
While I linger by thy side,
  Sweet Ellen Bayne!

Dream not in anguish,
  Dream not in fear,
Love shall not languish—
  Fond one's are near.
Sleeping or waking,
  In pleasure or pain,

Warm hearts will beat for thee,
　Sweet Ellen Bayne!
Gentle slumbers 'er thee glide,
Dreams of beauty round thee bide,
While I linger by thy side,
　Sweet Ellen Bayne!

Scenes that have vanished
　Smile on thee now—
Pleasures, once banished,
　Play round thy brow—
Forms long departed,
　Greet thee again,
Soothing thy dreaming heart,
　Sweet Ellen Bayne!
Gentle slumbers o'er thee glide,
Dreams of beauty round thee bide,
While I linger by thy side,
　Sweet Ellen Bayne!

LAKE OF KILLARNEY.

On the Lake of Killarney I first saw the lad
Who with song and with bagpipe could make my heart glad
And his hair was so red, and his eyes were so bright,
That they shone like the stars on a cold frosty night;
For tall and straight my dear Paddy was seen,
And he looked like the fairies that dance on the green.
Oh! the girls of Killarney wore the green willow tree
When first my dear Patrick sung love tales to me,
And he sung and he danced, and he won my fond heart,
To save his dear life, with my own I would part.

MARY OF ARGYLE.

I have heard the mavis singing
　His love song to the morn;
I have seen the dewdrop clinging
　To the rose just newly born:
But a sweeter song has cheered me
　At the evening's gentle close,
And I've seen an eye still brighter
　Than the dewdrops on the rose,

4

'Twas thy voice, my gentle Mary,
And thy artless winning smile,
That has made this world an Eden,
Bonnie Mary of Argyle.

Though thy voice may lose its sweetness,
And thine eye its brightness too—
Though thy step may lose its fleetness,
And thy hair its sunny hue—
Still to me shalt thou be dearer
Than all the world can own;
I have loved thee for thy beauty,
But not for that alone,
I have watch'd thy heart, dear Mary,
And its goodness was the wile
That has made me thine forever,
Bonnie Mary of Argyle.

LAND OF KING COTTON.

Air—*Red, White and Blue.*

Oh! Dixie the land of King Cotton,
The home of the brave and the free;
A nation by Freedom begotten,
The terror of despots to be;
Wherever thy banner is streaming,
Base tyranny quails at thy feet,
And Liberty's sunlight is beaming,
In splendor of majesty sweet.
Three cheers for our army so true,
Three cheers for Price, Johnston and Lee,
Beauregard and our Davis forever;
The pride of the brave and the free!

When Liberty sounds her war rattle,
Demanding her right and her due,
The first land that rallies to battle
Is Dixie the shrine of the true;
Thick as leaves of the forest in summer,
Her brave sons will rise on each plain;
And then strike, until each vandal comer
Lies dead on the soil he would stain.
Three cheers for our army, &c.

May the names of the dead that we cherish,
  Fill memory's cup to the brim ;
May the laurels they've won never perish,
  Nor "star of their glory grow dim;"
May the States of the South never sever,
  But the champions of freedom e'er be,
May they flourish, Confed'rate forever,
  The boast of the brave and the free.
    Three cheers for our army so true,
      Three cheers for Price, Johnston and Lee,
    Beauregard and our Davis forever;
      The pride of the brave and the free !

THE CAPTURE OF LEXINGTON.

Air—*The Old Oaken Bucket.*

'Twas during September, we drove in the Federal,
At Lexington city, in the State of old Pike,
Our brave General said, " now, my boys, hit them central,
We'll give them our bullets, many more than they like."
We surrounded the town, with our brave, gallant band, sir,
Determined to take them *all*, let not one get away,
McBride and brave Green stormed with rifle in hand, sir,
And many a Fed bit the dust on that day.
    Three cheers for our General, who drove in the Federal,
    Cornered them, took them in this Lexington town.

Colonel Mulligan was there with his Irish Brigade, sir,
All the way from Chicago, in the State of Illinois,
These Irishmen fought like true, brave men indeed, sir,
Being commanded and governed by such a brave boy.
They had thrown up intrenchments and ditches in number,
They had dug up the earth in magnificent style,
Had hidden provisions and other such lumber,
And made preparations to stay a good while.
    Three cheers for our General, who drove in the Federal,
    Cornered them, took them in this Lexington town.

Somebody told PRICE of the "Hemp" that was near by,
We got it, and wet it, and rolled it up hill;
Our "rifles" behind this good hemp line, hid thereby,
Knocked off the top-knots of the Feds at their will—
" What the devil does this mean ?" the Irishmen said, sir ;
Poor Mulligan was puzzled to death at the sight,

In all of his reading, he never had read, sir,
Of anything like this *hemp fort* on his right.
Three cheers for our General, who drove in the Federal,
Cornered them, took them in this Lexington town.

Three days and three nights did our boys bold their ground, si
'Mid battle's wild rage and the cannon's loud blast,
The news spread abroad o'er the country around, sir,
That Mulligan had surrendered to STERLING at last.
Thirty-two hundred we took, and their arms too;
Our victory was perfect, but we did it up nice,
We had saved our dear homes, and our ladies' bright charms to
And all this was owing to brave STERLING PRICE.
Nine cheers for our General, who drove in the Federal,
And captured the army of Lexington town.

THE JOLLY BACHELOR.

I am a jolly bachelor,
　So hearty, hale, and free,
What people wish to marry for,
　Is more than I can see,
I would not be a married man,
　For woman, wit, or money,
Or the responsibilities,
　That come with matrimony.
　So now young ladies!
　　Oh! don't you wait for me,
　For I'll be a bachelor
　　So hearty, hale, and free.

Once in my boyish days, I know,
　Of love I used to dream,
A certain pretty girl in shorts,
　An angel then did seem,
'She's married now—I saw her, but
　A single year ago—
Her foot was on the cradle, and
　Her hand was in the dough.

Here's John, and Ned, and Charlie too—
　Have knelt before the altar,
And carelessly have slipped their necks,
　Into the marriage halter;
For care and toil and curtain talk,

Of life they've sold their lease,
And wives, you know, can never mend
The breaches of their peace.

Oh, 'tis a sorry sight to see,
One strive a wife to win,
For, like the lilies of the vale,
They neither toil nor spin;
With talk they break your peaceful rest,
They scold the livelong day,
And sometimes with your handsome friend
They take themselves away.

You may have heard ot M-s. Lot,
Who, for a woman's fau t,
Was changed into a pillar of
The best Turk s Island salt;
It saved her husband then, but now
We many a husband have.
Whom. far beyond such remedy,
No salt would ever save.

I knew a "nice young lady" once,
As lovely as a saint,
Her cheeks were red as roses, though
I rather think with paint,
She used to sing enchantingly,
Was quiet as a kitten,
I popped the question to her, and
For answer got the mitten.

She married Fitz Roy Flash, Esquire,
A member of the bar,
He thought he'd got an angel, and
She fancied him a star;
They quarrelled, he forsook the law
For whi key, cards, and stout—
Poor Mrs. Flash makes bonnets now,
And Fitz Roy Flash flashed out.

But I am happy all the time,
No one to ask me when
I come home rather late at night,
"My dear, where have you been?"
And when I seek my quiet bed,
Untouched by care or strife,
I'd rather sink into the arms
Of Morpheus, than a wife.

NOBODY'S BOY.

The flowers of spring have passed away,
   And winter's chilling blasts have come;
I'm here alone a helpless lad,
   Without a friend, without a home.
My tattered garments scarce conceal,
   From vulgar gaze, each shivring limb;
My aching heart is pierced with cold,
   And tears of grief my eyes bedim.
     The days are few since I was called
       My father's pride, my mother's joy;
     But oh! those days will ne'er return,
     For now, alas! I'm nobody's boy.

My heart doth yearn for that dear home,
   Where I so oft upon the hearth
Have sat beside the gleaming fire,
   And mingled in gay scenes of mirth;
But little dreamed I in those days,
   When all was joy within that cot,
That I so young would thus be left
   And this world be my gloomy lot.
     The days are few, &c.

I mourn the loss of parents kind,
   And cherished friends, to me most dear,
For, since of them I am bereft,
   There's none to guard when danger's near,
There's none on earth the place can fill
   Of that dear one who gave me birth;
Then ask not why I shed these tears,
   And cease to join in scenes of mirth.
     The days are few, &c.

POP GOES THE WEASEL.

The painter works with ladder and brush,
   The artist with the easel,
The fiddler always snaps the string
   At pop goes the weasel.
   From round about the countryman's barn
   The mice begin to mizzle;
For, when they poke their noses out,
   Pop goes the weasel.

The butcher, when he charges for meat,
   Sticks in the bones and grizzel,
But that's the way the money goes,
   And pop goes the weasel.
From round about, &c.

Potatoes for an Irishman's taste,
   A doctor for the measles,
A fiddler always for a dance,
   Or pop goes the weasel.
From round about, &c.

Blood pudding for a Dutchman's meal,
   A workman for a chisel,
The tune that everybody sings
   Is pop goes the weasel.
From round about, &o.

———————

JOHNNIE JORDAN.

I came from the east,
   I went to the west
To hunt for a house for to board in,
   And I soon found a rest,
   When I dressed in my best,
And put down my name as Johnie Jordan.
      So I took off my coat,
         And I rolled up my sleeves,
   And I made myself at home accordin',
      For when a fellow's tired,
         He generally leaves,
   And so does the legs of Johnnie Jordan, I believe.

         They served four kinds of meat,
         When the boarders came to eat,
'Twas sheep, ram, lamb, and mutton;
         So I tried to eat a slice,
         For it look'd so mighty nice;
But I couldn't if I'd been an awful glutton:
         I said I had enough,
            for it was mighty tough,
That I could not eat the piece I chanc'd on:
            the landlord took the bread,
            struck me on the head,
And black the eye of Johnny Jordan.
         Then I took off my coat, &c.

The landlord said, "Oh, no!
Young man, you cannot go,
You cannot leave this house until you poney;
And I'll hit an awful smash
On that curly calabash,
If you don't plank down with your money."
He kept a skinny horse,
And a dog so mighty cross,
With a broad brass collar with a cord on;
He caught me by the hip,
When out I thought to slip,
And nearly was the death of Johnnie Jordon:
Then I took off my coat,
And I rolled up my sleeves,
And I made myself at home accordin',
For, when a fellow's tired,
He generally leaves,
And so does the legs of Johnnie Jordan, I believe.

———————

BOBBING AROUND.

In August last, on one fine day,
A bobbing around, around, around,
When Josh and I went to make hay,
We were bobbing around.

Says Josh to me let's take a walk,
A bobbing around, around, around,
Then we can have a talk,
As we go bobbing around.

We walk'd along to the mountain ridge,
A bobbing around, around, around,
Til we got near Squire Slipshop's bridge,
As we went bobbing around.

Then Josh and I went on a spree,
A bobbing around, around, around,
And I kissed Josh, and Josh kiss'd me,
As we went bobbing around.

Then Josh's pluck longer tarried,
A bobbing a round, around,
Says he dear i e's get married,
Then w t n ud.

Now I knew he lov'd another gal,
. A bobbing around, around, around,
They call'd her long legg'd, crook'd shin, curly
   tooth'd, Sal,
 When he went bobbing around.

So after we got into church,
 A bobbing around, around, around,
I cut and left Josh in the lurch,
 Then he went bobbing around.

So all you chaps what's got a gal,
 A bobbing around, around, around,
·Do think of long legg'd, crook'd shin, curly
   tooth'd Sal, ·
 When you go bobbing around.

NANCY TILL.

Down in the cane brake, close by the mill,
There lived a gal, and her name was Nancy Till;
She know'd that I loved her, she know'd it long,
 I'm going to serenade her, and Ill sing this song.
  Come, love, come! the boat lies low,
  She lies high and dry on the Ohio;
  Come, love, come! won't you go along with me,
  I'll row the boat, while the boat rows me.

Open the window love, oh, do!
And listen to the music I'm playing for you.
The whisperings of love so soft and low
Harmonize my voice with the old banjo.
  Come, love, come! the boat lies low, .
  She lies high and dry on the Ohio;
  Come, love, come! won't you go with me,
  I'll row the boat, while the boat rows me.·

Softly the casement began for to rise,
The stars am a shining above in the skies;
 moon is declining behind yonder hill
Reflecting its rays on you, my Nancy Till.
  Come, love, come! the boat lies low,
  She lies high and dry on the Ohio;
 , Come, love, come! won't you go along with me,
  I'll row the boat, while the boat rows me.

Farewell, love! I now must away,
I've a long way to travel before the break of day,
But the next time I come, be ready for to go
A sailing oh the banks of the Ohio.
Come, love, come! the boat lies low,
She lies high and dry on the Ohio;
Come, love, come! won't you go with me,
I'll row the boat, while the boat rows me.

I SEEN HER AT THE WINDOW.

Last night I went to Dinah's house, to see if my lub has been dar,
I cast my eyes up at de house, and saw her at the window;
So in I went to see my dear, and met her sister 'Manda,
Dey was seated around the fire-place, pickin' de old gray gander.
  I seen her at de window,
   'Twas my dear Lucinda;
   She dress'd so neat, and look'd so sweet,
   I'd gib my life to bin in dar.

I took a seat down by my lub, and we talked about the matter,
I axed her if she'd marry me, but her mudder wouldn't let her;
I told her if she'd run away, I'd take her down de ribber,
I'd gib her all de money I had, likewise my heart forever.
  I seen her at de window,
   'Twas my dear Lucinda;
   She dress'd so neat, and look'd so sweet,
   I'd gib my life to bin in dar.

Dar was a darkie by the name of Joe, who long did lub dis lady,
He serenaded her at night, and like to set her crazy;
I found she loved music so, and I had often been dar,
I'd sing all night, wid de old banjo, "I seen her at de window."
  I seen her at de window,
   'Twas my dear Lucinda;
   She dress'd so neat, and look'd so sweet,
   I'd gib my life to bin in dar.

My lub and me hab both turned one, an mean to lib togeth
No darkie now can part us. for we're tied de not foreber;
So white gents, if you want a gal, and see her at de window,
Go dat night and serenade. and I bet my life you get in dar.
  I seen her at de window,
   'Twas my dear Lucinda;
   She dress'd so neat and look'd so sweet,
   I'd gib my life to bin in dar.

BACHELOR'S HALL.

Bachelor's Hall, what a queer looking place it is,
    Keep me from such all the days of my life;
Sure I think what a burning disgrace it is,
    Never at all to be getting a wife.
See the old bachelor fretting and sad enough,
    Placing his tay-kettle over the fire;
Soon tips it over, St. Patrick is mad enough,
    If he were present, to fight with the squire.

Now, like a hog in the mortar bed wallowing,
    Awkward enough to see him kneading his dough;
Truth, if the bread he could eat without swallowing
    How it would favor his palate you know.
Pots, dishes, pans, a d such greasy commodities,
    Ashes and pratey skins kiver the floor;
His cupboard's a store-house of comical oddities,
    Things that had never been neighbors before.

His meal being over, his table left sitting so,
    Dishes take care of yourselves if you can;
Hunger returns, then he's fuming and fretting so,
    Oh! let him alone for a baste of a man.
Late in the night, when he goes to bed shivering,
    Never a bit is the bed made at all,
He crapes like a terrapin under the kivering;
    Bad luck to the picture of Bachelor's Hall.

- LONG, LONG AGO.

Tell me the tales that to me were so dear,
    Long, long ago—long, long ago;
Sing me the songs I delighted to hear
    Long, long ago—long a
Now you are come all my grief is removed,
Let me forget that so long you have roved,
Let me believe that you love you loved,
    Long, long ago—long ago.

Do you remember the path where we met,
    Long, long ago long, long ago?
Ah! yes, you told me you ne'er would forget,
    Long, long ago—long ago.
Then to all other my smile you preferr'd,

Love, when you spoke, gave a charm to each word;
Still my heart treasures the praises I heard,
    Long, long ago—long ago.

Though your kindness my fond hopes were raised,
    Long, long ago—long, long ago,
You, by more eloquent lips, have been raised,
    Long, long ago—long ago.
But by long absence your truth has been tried,
Still to your accents I listen with pride,
Blest as I was when I sat by your side,
    Long, long ago—long ago.

MY MOTHER DEAR.

There was a place in childhood that I remember well,
And there a voice of sweetest tone bright fairy tales did tell,
And gentle words and fond embrace were given with joy to me,
When I was in that happy place, upon my mother's knee.
    My mother dear! my mother dear!
    My gentle, gentle mother!

When fairy tales were ended, "good night" she softly said,
And kiss'd and laid me down to sleep within my tiny bed,
And holy words she taught me there—methinks I yet can see
Her angel eyes as close I knelt beside my mother's knee.
    Oh mother dear! my mother dear!
    My gentle, gentle mother!

In the sickness of my childhood, the perils of my prime,
The sorrows of my riper years, the cares of ev'ry time—
When doubt or danger weigh'd me down, then pleading all for me,
It was a fervent prayer to heaven that bent my mother's knee.
    My mother dear! my mother dear!
    My gentle, gentle mother!

YOUNG WIDOW

She is neat, she is bashful.
    Free and easy but not bold—
Like an apple ripe and mellow.
    Not too young, not too old,

Half inviting, half repulsing,
  Now advancing and now shy,
There is mischief in her dimple,
  There is danger in her eye.

She has studied human nature,
  She is schooled in all her arts,
She has taken her degree
  As the mistress of all hearts.
She can tell the very moment
  When to sigh and when to smile;
Oh! a maid is sometimes charming,
  But a widow all the while.

You are sad? how very serious
  Will her handsome face become;
Are you angry? she is wretched,
  Lonely, friendless, tearful dumb.
Are you mirthful? how her laughter,
  Silver sounding, will ring out;
She can lure, and catch, and play you
  As the angler does the trout.

Ye old bachelors of forty
  Who have grown so bold and wise,
Young Americans of twenty,
  With your lovelocks in your eyes,
You may practice all the lessons
  Taught by Cupid since the fall,
But I know a little widow,
  Who could win and fool you all.

THE WATCHER.

The night was dark and fearful,
  The blast swept wailing by;
A watcher, pale and tearful,
  Look'd forth with anxious eye.
How wistfully she gazeth!
  No gleam of morn is there,
Her eyes to heav'n she raiseth
  In agony of prayer.

Within that dwelling lonely,
  Whe e want and darkness reign,
 Her precious child—her only—
  Lay moaning in his pain,
And death alone can free him;
  She feels that it must be—
" But oh ! for morn to see him
  Smile once again on me."

A hundred lights are gleaming
  In yonder mansion fair,
And merry feet are dancing :
  They heed not mourning there.
Oh ! gay and joyous creatures,
  One lamp from out your store
Would give that poor boy's features
  To his mother's gaze once more.

The morning sun is shining,
  She heedeth not its ray ;
Beside her dead reclining
  The pale dead mother lay.
A smile her lips was wreathing,
  A smile of hope and love,
As though she still were breathing
  " There's light for us above."

_____

KEMO KIMO.

Away down South, where I was born,
  Sing song, Kitty, Kitty Kimeo,
I chop de wood and busk de corn,
  And sing all day of Kitty Kimeo.
Kemo Kimo is de tune
    De darkeys sing from morn till noon,
  Singing Kemo Kimo all day long,
    For Kemo Kimo is de song.

Come, my lub, and go wid me,
  Sing song, Kitty, Kitty Kimeo,
I'll take you down in the country,
  Sing song, Kitty, Kitty Kimeo.
Kemo Kimo is de tune
    De darkeys sing from morn till noon,
  Singing Kemo Kimo all day long,
    For Kemo Kimo is de song.

Now white folks, we e a gwine away,
 Sing song, Kitty, Kitty Kimeo,
Sing for you some ol er day,
 Sing song, Kitty Kitty Kimeo.
  Kemo Kimo is de une
    De darkeys sing from morn till noon,
  - Singing Kemo-Ki , all day long,
    For Kemo Kim s de song.

ALL THINGS LOVE THEE—SO DO I.

Gentle waves upon the deep
 Murmur soft when thou dost sleep;
Little birds upon the tree,
 Sing their sweetest songs for e.

Cooling gales with voices low
 In the tree-tops gent y blow;
When thou dost in slumbers lie,
 All things love thee so do I.

When thou wak d th see will pour
 Treasures on thee to the shore;
And the earth in plant and tree
 Bring forth fruit and flowers for thee.

Whilst the glorious stars above
 Shine on thee like trusting love;
When thou dost in slumber lie,
 All things love thee—so do I!

THE SAILOR'S RETURN.

With hope, as land appears,
 The seaman's heart is bounding;
The village bell he hears,
 Yet knows not why 'tis sounding.

Tis there a maiden dwells,
 To him her troth was plighted;
That sound too plainly tells
 They ne'er can be united.

Some youth with fairer form
  A willing bride doth wed her;
Or, in a lover's place,
  Death to the grave hath led her.

Whoe'er the bride hath won,
  He now from her must sever,
He feels that joy is gone
  From his sad heart forever.

Her well-known home once more
  He views with soft emotion,
Then steers his boat from shore,
  And seeks the stormy ocean.

www.ingramcontent.com/pod-product-compliance
Lightning Source LLC
Chambersburg PA
CBHW021525090426
42739CB00007B/779